I0487403

The Voyage East

The Voyage East

An Executives' Guide to Offshore Outsourcing

Prashant Dubey

iUniverse, Inc.

New York Lincoln Shanghai

The Voyage East
An Executives' Guide to Offshore Outsourcing

All Rights Reserved © 2003 by Prashant Dubey

No part of this book may be reproduced or transmitted in any form or by any means, graphic, electronic, or mechanical, including photocopying, recording, taping, or by any information storage retrieval system, without the written permission of the publisher.

iUniverse, Inc.

For information address:
iUniverse
2021 Pine Lake Road, Suite 100
Lincoln, NE 68512
www.iuniverse.com

ISBN: 0-595-28834-0 (Pbk)
ISBN: 0-595-65890-3 (Cloth)

Printed in the United States of America

To the memory of my father,
Professor Sumati Narain Dubey

ACKNOWLEDGEMENTS

I would like to thank my Norwegian wife Sarah, for reminding me that good ideas are only good when they are acted upon.

Furthermore, I would like to thank Sarah for allowing me to continue my multi-cultural aspirations through my progeny.

I would also like to thank my Norwindian sons Shanti and Narain for just reminding me….

CONTENTS

INTRODUCTION

VOY·AGE:

*a course (as a series of actions or sequence of events)
leading in a direction or toward an objective*

1: an act or instance of traveling

2: a course or period of traveling

3: an account of a journey

For many of us, the term "voyage" might conjure up images of the fifteenth century Portuguese explorer, Vasco da Gama or of the legendary misguided discoverer, Christopher Columbus. These images are fraught with unpredictability, danger, adventure, excitement, fulfillment, intricate human dynamics, disease, achievement, accolades, vision and sometimes even—conquest.

Voyages are undertaken, even in the 21st century. The difference between these and 15th Century voyages is that, today, the technical and operational aspects of the voyage are rarely an issue. All the tools to make the voyage safe are readily available. The expertise and experience to ensure that the proper destination is reached is plentiful. Even the weather can be managed with satellite technology and global positioning systems. The most challenging issues are no longer the operational. The issues we deal with in the 21st Century are primarily emotional.

VASCO DA GAMA: "NO-MAN OR NOBLEMAN?"

In 1498 a Portuguese nobleman and explorer, Vasco da Gama set sail from Portugal, headed south around the Cape of Good Hope, passed Kenya and reached the west coast of India. During the journey, he solicited help from an Arab navigator to find land (which he lost sight of twice, for ninety days). In addition to these operational errors, da Gama also was not sure what he was searching for. The high level reason for the voyage was "to serve God and create monetary profits." How the voyage would actually contribute to that, was never clear. Upon arrival in India, da Gama thought the locals were Christians of some sort and their temples were some type of Churches. He only stayed in India for a few months.

Vasco da Gama returned to India twice, each time, plundering and demanding the extradition of various constituents. There is much 21st Century discourse about the rationale behind this behavior—some believe it was in the name of Christianity, others believe it was in the name of wealth acquisition. Vasco da Gama was eventually appointed Viceroy of Portuguese India but died 3 months after his appointment, on Christmas Eve. Today, many believe that da Gamas' arrival in India marked the advent of an era of repressive and destructive colonialism. Vasco da Gama mis-read all the cultural cues of the time, never figured out how to assimilate in India and therefore never was able to fulfill his stated goals of serving God and creating profits. Essentially, da Gama was remembered neither as a great man, nor as a nobleman.

FEAR OF A VASCO-ECTOMY

If you are an executive who is a relatively new entrant into the world of offshore technology outsourcing, the mis-steps of Vasco da Gama are possibly your greatest trepidation. In a 21st century, U.S. corporate context, these fears are not as severe as the "fear of pillage and plunder." However, it is highly likely that you engage in plentiful dialog around issues related to the reasons for "going offshore", the cultural assimilation that needs to occur, the fear of working with a people thousands of miles away, who by virtue of their lack of geographic proximity—"must behave differently." If these conversations do not occur with others, then there is a high probability that they occur in your own mind. In addition, you are probably concerned about the underlying "unpredictability of outcome." The principle of "if it isn't broken, don't fix it," is accompanied by "if it is broken, fix it—with a known solution." You wonder whether offshore outsourcing is enough of a known solution.

There are also emotional fears that are internalized as operational fears. For example, my numerous conversations with executives have revealed a lot of anxiety about which partner/guide to select for the offshore voyage and what the geographic destination of the journey should be (to meet the business objective)? How should one reconcile the nationalist fervor surrounding "saving American jobs" with the business rationale that points us toward offshore technology outsourcing? These are, at their core, emotional issues. However, they manifest themselves operationally, in mechanisms like the Request for Proposal (RFP) document you construct, the overall partner/vendor selection process you put in place, the contracts you eventually sign and the way you measure the Return On Offshore (ROO) once your partner has begun their work.

Depending on how you manage the emotional dimension of the offshore outsourcing decision, you will either be operationally fluid, or operationally overindulgent. One of the key objectives of this guide is to simplify the transition of the emotional dimension into operational elements that are easy to understand, easy to execute and easy to measure.

INDIA AS THE DESTINATION FOR THE VOYAGE EAST

Offshore outsourcing is different from near-shore outsourcing. From a U.S. perspective, near-shore is considered Canada or Mexico. The only similarities (from a technology outsourcing perspective) between these two countries are the facts that they both share a land border with the United States and they are both in the Western Hemisphere of the globe, (rather than the Eastern Hemisphere). From a technology outsourcing perspective, these countries have seen some increase in business coming their way from the U.S., however they are both still relatively small players in the global marketplace for information technology services.

This guide is derived from the experience and expertise of individuals that have been stalwarts in the offshore outsourcing business for decades. These experts have all been associated with offshore technology outsourcing with India as the offshore destination. The principles outlined in this guide are geography agnostic, however, there is an implicit bias in the writing of this guide. That bias is that, as of the publishing of this guide, India is the dominant country for offshore technology outsourcing. Here are some of the facts to consider:

- In 2003, the Information Technology (IT) market in India will grow 19%—from $4.7 Billion. to $5.5 Billion

- Estimates state that by 2005, the IT market in India will reach $11.5 Billion.

- Outsourcing companies with offshore technology operations in India are no longer positioned as rudimentary programming and code generation factories. These organizations have Application Outsourcing, Infrastructure Outsourcing, Data Center Operation, Business Process Outsourcing and Strategic IT

Consulting as their core competencies. Even new software package installation, IT Strategy and Research and Development are being performed by offshore organizations in India.

- India has had a direct impact on the IT industry in the U.S. In the heyday of the Internet boom, 40% of all high-tech startups in the Silicon Valley (the "Valley") were spawned by Indians.

- More than half of the Indian spawned start-ups in the Valley were started by Indian Institute of Technology (IIT) graduates. 30% of IIT graduates are wooed to the United States for post-graduate education.

- IIT graduates have become part of the fabric of the executive suite in the United States. The founder of Sun Microsystems, and the Managing Partner of McKinsey & Company, are of Indian descent—and IIT graduates.

• Recently, the need for these talented IIT graduates to leave India has diminished. Employment opportunities with attractive pay exist in India. As a result, the talent stays, and US companies using India for offshore outsourcing are assured that they are not merely getting access to "cheap labor." The level of talent available in India today, is unprecedented.

There are many other statistics that can be quoted. However, the best mechanism to determine India's role in the IT outsourcing marketplace is to poll CIO's that have been using offshore resources for more than a decade. Almost all of these CIO's have relationships with companies that have offshore operations in India. At least for now, India appears to be leading the world market for IT outsourcing services.

APPLICATION OUTSOURCING

This guide focuses on Application Outsourcing (AO). The technology-outsourcing continuum contains everything from infrastructure outsourcing to Business Process Outsourcing (BPO) to Strategic IT Portfolio Management. However, the bulk of corporate IT resources (hard dollars as well as human resources) are expended on developing and maintaining software applications. As such, this guide is focused on Application Maintenance & Development (AMD) outsourcing, which falls under the umbrella concept of Application Outsourcing. Many of the elements outlined in this guide are transferable to any offshore technology outsourcing decision, but the nuances of things such as call center outsourcing or data center operations are not directly addressed.

THE ESSENCE OF THIS GUIDE

Offshore outsourcing is like a voyage in that reaching the destination is only part of the conquest. Preparation for the voyage is a crucial element. Coming to terms with the rationale behind embarking on the voyage is often an arduous process. Selecting your guide/partner for the voyage can be a nerve-wracking experience.

This guide is meant to offer not just perspective on these challenges, but also some experiential approaches to traverse the key steps in an offshore application outsourcing partnership. This partnership starts with understanding the business drivers behind a decision to "go offshore" and then outlines how to establish a lucid strategy for the offshore voyage and concludes with a section on how to select the best partner (voyage guide.). Along the way, you will also be able to get ideas of how to incorporate the approaches suggested, into your operational processes for "going offshore." These are the key elements in making an offshore technology outsourcing decision.

Fundamentally, this guide is not meant to be an elixir. It does not provide Request for Proposal (RFP) templates or models to calculate Return on Investment (ROI). These items can easily be accessed from a multitude of sources—including from your potential partners. Rather, the essence of this guide is perspective. With perspective, comes under-standing. With understanding comes rational thinking. With rational thinking, comes rational decision-making. And all of us could use more of that.

Welcome to the Voyage East.

**Note: the terms Application Outsourcing, offshore outsourcing and off-shore technology outsourcing are used interchangeably in this guide.

CHAPTER 1

GOAL OF THE VOYAGE

Vasco da Gama went searching for God and for profits. In a general sense, this is a well-defined goal. However, some historians have theorized that Vasco da Gama only had God and profits as his goals because that is what noblemen of the time (who were also explorers) were expected to desire.

da Gamas' mis-steps upon his arrival in India and subsequent "colonization" of the western region of Goa were not necessarily supportive of his goals. He alienated reigning monarchs by presenting them inadequate gifts and extradited Muslims while systematically eliminating many constituencies that did not fit his objectives. He left, a beaten man, returning to India 21 years later as the Viceroy of Portuguese India and wanting to make amends by setting up trading pacts (purportedly to achieve profits) and downplaying colonialism. Unfortunately, da Gama died shortly after his arrival, on Christmas Eve.

In addition to not being able to live out his tenure as Viceroy, today, 500 years later, his effigies are being burned in Goa and he is being denounced as a brutal colonialist and butcher. He left a legacy of brutality, misunderstanding and hatred. It can be argued, that, in the end, da Gama never achieved his goal.

HAVING A GOAL IS NOT ENOUGH

As you explore offshore outsourcing it is crucial that you establish lucid goals for your voyage. In addition, as da Gamas' follies teach us, it is not enough to merely have well articulated goals. The goals must be consistent with the operational aspects of your offshore voyage and must be aligned with your organization's objectives overall.

It is important that your goal is not set based on what you think you **should** have as your goal. Your goal for offshore might be dramatically different than your peers in the industry and even from what you read in the popular press. God and profits seem to be worthy goals, but can create dysfunction in the voyage if they are established merely because there is an expectation that these should be the goals.

One of the most pervasive goals of offshore outsourcing seems to be operational cost reduction. The means to achieve this end is articulated simply as "lower labor costs," or "labor arbitrage." The problem with this overly simplistic goal is that it is usually established out of context with the organization's overall business situation and out of context with the IT organizations' challenges. So, how do you resolve this?

CREATE CONTEXT THROUGH INTRO-SPECTION

The first step in creating context is to realize that your IT organization is unique. Furthermore, the business situation of your company is unique and the trials and tribulations faced by the CIO and the IT organization are unique. This uniqueness does not mean that your situation is not replicated anywhere else.

It is being suggested that your IT organization is the only one that has **your** company's business challenges to internalize, **your** team's human dynamics to interweave into these challenges and **your** functional and technical challenges. The combination of these organizational factors is unique to you and therefore presents a unique context.

In order to establish context sensitive goals for your off-shore outsourcing voyage, you need to go through some introspection. This is not a yogic or a meditative exercise.

Rather it is a practical exercise that allows you to articulate goals for your voyage based on two things:

1. The level of resources that your IT organization has been provided and,

2. The expectation of output that the company has from IT.

These two factors viewed in a matrix fashion, results in the diagram in Figure 1. There are a few broad categories that can be used to group challenges faced by the IT organization. Internalizing your operational challenges by placing yourself in one of these categories is critical to the success of an offshore outsourcing voyage.

Essentially, **you need to know who you are** in order to successfully leverage offshore outsourcing. Who you are (as defined by your business situation), determines what goals you will have for your offshore outsourcing voyage. Figure

1 outlines the 3 categories of CIOs/IT organizations as defined by their business challenges.

FIGURE 1

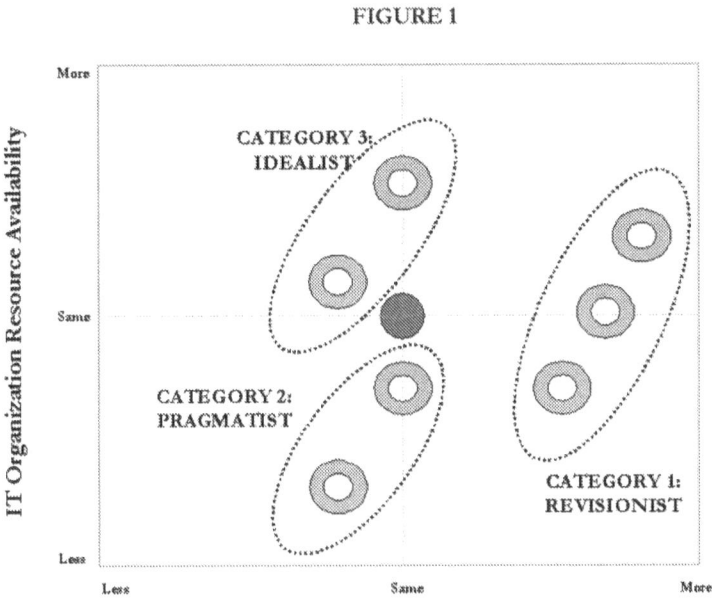

CATEGORY 3: IDEALIST

It is highly unlikely, in today's economic climate, that you are an idealist. Most likely, you are aspiring to be…an idealist. An idealist is a CIO/IT/Development organization that has been granted more resources (dollars!!!) to produce the **same or less** output than prior periods. While considering the low probability of this scenario we (briefly) yearn for the irrational exuberance of 1997—2001.

Though it is highly unlikely that you are an idealist, it is still possible. You may have been starved for resources while the customer facing organizations were being augmented. Marketing might have been over-funded to support the sales organization. Your company might have been taking a "harvest" strategy, trying to penetrate the market and retain customers with the existing business systems and hoping enhancements, round-the-clock user support and application development would continue despite no investment.

You may have been stretching your system administrators and application portfolio managers and promising them that, "better times are yet to come."

Better times may have arrived, and the company may have just granted you resources appropriate for the output expected. Or better yet, the company has realized that your team has been "burning the candle at both ends" and needs relief. So you get more resources and are expected to output less. If this is the case, great! You will finally be able to operate rationally.

THE IDEAL IDEALIST

As an idealist, presented with the opportunity to leverage offshore outsourcing, you will wonder how you can capitalize on the situation. One of the ways that other successful idealists (yes, there have been unsuccessful ones) have done this is to look at their entire portfolio of projects and initiatives holistically.

Which projects do your architects and developers really want to work on? Have your technocrats been doing rudimentary maintenance work while their desire is to work on new applications, technologies and architectures?

In this case, you can take your new found (yet badly needed) resources to partner with an external services provider to whom you can off-load some of the rudimentary work and allow your existing team to work on the "exciting" stuff. Idealists can take advantage of the rational allocation of resources to **produce more.**

Offshore outsourcing, with its built in labor cost efficiencies and process orientation, allows an idealist to increase efficiency and therefore effectiveness, even in times that seem flush with resources.

As an idealist, the articulation of the goal for your offshore outsourcing voyage is probably going to go something like this:

- Alleviate pressures on my in-house IT organization (and enhance morale) by off-loading rudimentary application maintenance work.

- Re-deploy my in-house personnel to more strategic endeavors.

- Help my development teams develop new applications by leveraging offshore to perform QA, testing or integration work.

- Augment my IT organization with skills that can be accessed with a short turnaround time.

The most important thing for you to remember is that, even idealists do not remain idealists forever. One of the best times to establish an offshore technology outsourcing partnership is when you are not being forced to do it. Idealists have the luxury, albeit short-lived, of being proactive about including offshore outsourcing as part of their overall IT strategy.

CATEGORY 2: PRAGMATIST

In today's economic climate, pragmatists are everywhere. You are a pragmatist if you have been **granted lower resources, but are expected to produce the same output and provide the same or greater support** as prior periods.

You can also be a pragmatist if you are expected to produce less due to a decrease in resources. However the reduction of resources is not in proportion to the reduction in expectation of output. Resources might be cut 30% but output expectation is only cut 10%, resulting in a much higher expectation of output.

THE PRAGMATISTS DILEMMA

Offshore outsourcing is a pragmatists' friend. Expectation of output takes on a quantity as well as a time dimension. Despite the expectation that IT spend will be reduced, pragmatists are still expected to upgrade applications rapidly, release new functionality on time and implement new business improvement initiatives like "single sign-on." There is a low level of tolerance for "functionality prioritization."

The sales and marketing organizations need the new version of the customer relationship management (CRM) system—yesterday. The head of manufacturing needs to put in place the new supply chain module or she will not be able to increase inventory turns. The CFO needs the new activity-based costing module up and running with all the data interfaces live—or customer profitability cannot be calculated and EBITDA (the finance acronym most often used by non-finance people trying to act knowledgeable) will be at risk.

The challenge for the IT executive, in this scenario, is **how and where** to reduce resources. Often, the resource reduction comes in the form of a "number" or "percentage" reduction. There is a rare CFO that will be prescriptive about the specific areas of IT that should be cut. The hard stuff is left to the line manager. However, expense reduction targets will happily be handed out by the CFO. The challenge to get "to the number" is one that the pragmatist needs to solve.

THE PEANUT-BUTTER APPROACH

If you are a pragmatist you may be tempted to take the "peanut-butter" approach to cost reduction. This means you would take your reduction percentage and apply it evenly to all functions within IT. Some reduction would be absorbed by the capital budget, some by the salary budget.

The problem is that activities, not people, consume cost. If staffing levels in certain functions are reduced, (without regard for the value addition of the function), the activities performed by the individuals that are part of the function, often still remain. So what should you do?

THE PRAGMATISTS' GOAL-SETTING FRAMEWORK

In order to avoid the dysfunction created by the peanut-butter approach, you need to look at the IT portfolio holistically. In the context of setting goals for offshore application outsourcing, the activities that consume cost need to be parsed-using a IT centric view-into maintenance, development or some sub-specialty under these functions.

You may be lucky if you have a cost accounting system that allows you to slice and dice your IT budget in a multi-dimensional way (of course, the data warehousing and business intelligence systems that provide this flexibility would have been built by the IT organization!)

Once this parsing is complete, you should organize your application portfolio around some high-level risk/return dimensions. You should label the applications in your portfolio **"strategic, or non-strategic"** and assess the **"health"** of each application (subjectively) as either **"stable, or un-stable."** Once this is done, you have a framework to determine which activities should be outsourced.

USING THE FRAMEWORK TO SET (PRAGMATIC) GOALS

Using an activity-centric dimension to view IT spend allows you to apply the organization's goals for IT to the budget. Since you (as a pragmatist) are expected to reduce cost, you probably have a sense of how the expectation of output manifests itself.

Which new initiatives will be scrapped? Can the business accept 12-hour help desk support on the CRM application instead of 24 x 7 support? Can the ERP upgrade be delayed until next quarter? Are we really still pursuing the "virtual marketplace" initiative planned last year?

Based on the answers to these types of questions, you will be able to determine which functional area of IT (maintenance or development) can absorb the greatest resource reduction and which areas need resources re-directed toward them.

The dimensions of 'business criticality' and 'application stability' will allow you to look at your application portfolio in terms of risk. For example, applications that end up being "un-stable and non-business critical," might be the first candidates for targeted cost reduction. These applications can benefit from becoming stable and if efforts to reduce cost of supporting these applications don't work out as planned, the "non-business critical" nature of the applications will result in minimal turbulence to the business (i.e. lower risk)

It is quite possible in this scenario, that you can reduce IT operating cost significantly by leveraging offshore out-sourcing while having a minimal impact on the organization. For example, if the maintenance of certain applications (labeled "unstable and non-business critical") is outsourced to an offshore partner (with a lower cost structure), the personnel associated with these activities might be re-deployed, or might naturally attrite over time.

Obviously, there will be some impact to the organization, but if the process above is followed, the staff reduction might be viewed as more rational.

As a pragmatist, the goals for your offshore outsourcing voyage might be articulated in a fashion similar to this:

- Reduce cost of maintaining un-stable, non-business critical applications
- Manage users' service level expectation for help desk support for all non-business critical applications. Utilize offshore partner to provide 12-hour e-mail help desk (and telephone for escalation).
- Lower costs of implementing a new performance management system. Re-deploy new software purchase funds from capital budget to offshore partner for custom development of performance management system.

Offshore outsourcing, if approached properly, can help a pragmatist establish goals for the offshore voyage that reduce cost but still meet expectations of output.

CATEGORY 1: REVISIONIST

Revisionists are the new trend in IT organizations. As a revisionist, you are expected to **output more**.

This output could be measured in terms of:

• new applications, new technologies, faster response time for user support, or in time to market.

• Market facing products that require IT support need to hit the market sooner.

• Applications that drive business processes need to be put into production faster, with more functionality.

• Applications need to support more users in more places around the globe.

• Applications need to have all the bugs fixed, need to be available all the time and contain all the functional enhancements that users want.

• Applications need to have more user-friendly interfaces.

- Data needs to be available in multiple forms—in real time.
- There needs to be single sign-on.
- The environment, within the network, remotely or in a wireless domain, needs to be completely secure.

All this needs to be done with the same or less resources.

Even in situations where incremental resources are granted, the resource increase is not in proportion to the increase in expectation of output. Revisionists are placed squarely in the critical path of the organizations' success. Much rides on you doing things right.

THE REVISIONIST VOYAGE— CONQUEST, NOT DISCOVERY

As a revisionist, you will probably set multi-dimensional goals for your offshore voyage. You will need to access skills in a variety of technical domains—rapidly. Time to market demands will make "follow-the-sun" development strategies very appealing-theoretically, doubling the speed at which products can be brought to market.

You will need to look at your portfolio of IT investments holistically, in a fashion similar to the pragmatist. However, you will also need to focus a lot of effort on new initiatives.

Pragmatists can still move forward—they just do it incrementally. As a revisionist, you will be expected to make quantum leaps—in technology as well as operational efficiency. Revisionists tend to face the innovators dilemma (how do you grow the revenue line while reducing the operating expense line?) more than any other leader in the organization. Revisionists are expected to embark on their voyage with the goal of conquering something, not merely discovering it.

SETTING CONQUEST-ORIENTED GOALS

Idealists, and sometimes even, pragmatists, can get away with using offshore application outsourcing in a transactional way. This means that they can parse out pieces of work that might have a defined beginning and end.

As an example, they might use offshore "vendors" to decommission old systems and install new systems. At the end of the engagement, the vendor and client might part ways. As a revisionist, you cannot really successfully indulge a transactional relationship with an offshore "vendor"—you must create a relationship with a "partner." Your needs are too great.

You need to set goals for your offshore voyage with the assumption that when the destination is reached, you will need to assimilate into the new territory, since you are, more than likely, there to stay. In this context, as a revisionist, you are likely to articulate your goals for your offshore voyage in the following manner:

- Establish a dedicated offshore development center (DDC) as an extension of my in-house application development team in order to speed time to market.

- Establish Virtual Capacity: Create a floating pool of resources with blended skill sets that can be accessed at any time. Commit to a baseline of FTE's with any variance above that number being billed to me. Utilize this resource to respond to business needs rapidly and speed time to market while managing my fixed/variable expense ratio.

- Create a "Build-Operate-Transfer" model. Contract with my offshore partner to build development capacity and operate it for a few years, after which I want the option to take over the capacity and "purchase" it from them. Use this vehicle to reduce my up-front capital investment but still drive initiatives that create top line growth.

- Outsource all application maintenance to my offshore partner so that my in-house team can focus on new strategic initiatives.
- Keep technical architecture work in-house and leverage the DDC for all application development.

Essentially, offshore outsourcing is one of the primary means that revisionists can use to output more. Whether the "more" is done with the same, less or greater resources, revisionists find that the offshore outsourcing voyage is a long-term partnership.

OVERINDULGE INTROSPECTION?

Though introspection is an important exercise to ensure that your goals for offshore are aligned with your business needs, it is possible to make too much of the process.

Essentially, there are two primary considerations: outputs and inputs. What are you expected to deliver and what resources have you been given in support of these expectations? If you can apply a relative scale to each of these considerations and get comfortable with picking a category (idealist, pragmatist or revisionist), you will be able to put your goals into context.

The process is fairly simple, and it should remain that way. The problem is that many executives approach offshore application outsourcing in a uni-dimensional way—and neglect the simple introspective exercise. As a result, their only goal for offshore outsourcing is to "reduce cost by accessing cheap labor." This approach is rarely successful.

CHAPTER 2

VOYAGE STRATEGIC PLAN

For purveyors of fine films, the modern version of "The Titanic" was one of the most awe-inspiring tales of a voyage gone awry. The Titanic was a magnificent ship. The creators of the vessel had a fantastic goal—to make a ship that was the largest vessel ever to navigate the open seas with accommodations so luxurious that even kings and queens would feel at home. The goal was bold and probably even appropriate.

The main issue with the goal set by the architects of The Titanic was that they did not carry their goal (objective) all the way through the performance management hierarchy of:

- Objective
- Strategy
- Tactic
- Milestone

The creators of the Titanic stopped at the objective. Something can only be a rational objective if it can be measured. How else will you know if you have achieved the objective? Objectives drive strategies. Strategies allow you to make your objectives actionable. Tactics drive strategy and milestones ensure that your tactics get executed. However, it all starts with a strategic plan that supports the achievement of stated objectives. Avoid the iceberg.

TRANSLATING OBJECTIVES INTO STRATEGY

Chapter 1 outlined how you can introspect and use the results of the exercise to establish lucid objectives for your offshore voyage. In addition, it was determined that objectives are context sensitive (driven by your specific business situation). It follows that if objectives are context sensitive, so are strategies.

Strategic plans are different from operating plans. One of the primary differences between these two is the timeframe of planning. Operating plans, more often than not, are bounded by the budgeting timeframe. In the U.S. commercial sector that is usually twelve months, and in the U.S. public sector, it is usually twenty-four months. A decade ago, U.S. firms were putting ten and twenty year strategic plans in place, trying to emulate some of the successes of our Japanese colleagues. Today, however, with the rapid pace of technological and market change, strategic plans rarely exceed the three to five year timeframe, with most strategic plans focusing on a three year planning horizon.

A strategic plan for your offshore voyage should invoke a similar time horizon. As such, your objectives should also be articulated so that their achievement can be ultimately seen, at the end of a three-year period.

THREE-YEAR HORIZON

Why three years? Experience has shown that as you scale up your partnership with an offshore technology out-sourcer, there are distinct phases that your organization will go through in order to "operationalize" the partnership.

In the initial stages of scale-up, your partner will go through a knowledge acquisition phase. After that, the transition of management responsibility to a blended service delivery model using onsite/offsite/offshore resources will begin. Steady-state offshore operations do not kick in until a few months after the beginning of a partnership. At this point, any operational cost savings you expect start becoming tangible and measurable. However, your objectives are not yet achieved.

Your objectives for the offshore voyage most probably contain expectations for productivity improvements that go beyond the one time cost reduction achieved through labor arbitrage. These productivity improvements might include systems that run more efficiently (possibly measured by CPU utilization) or application errors being resolved faster. They might focus on technical factors such as a reduction in the total Lines of Code (LOC) or reduction of inventory levels due to field expansion work done on the stock-keeping numbers of your products.

These productivity improvements occur over a longer horizon and experience shows that it is usually rational to put productivity goals in place in three-year increments. This allows enough time for improvements to be made incrementally so that there is not a shock to the system and also allows you to distribute resources appropriately between operational improvements and new application development.

Lastly, in order to ensure that you do not create a transactional relationship with a strategic partner, like an offshore application outsourcing company, you need to give them time to produce results. A three-year planning horizon gives both you and your partner a chance to let your working relationship thrive.

THE OPTIMAL STRATEGY

There are many opinions about the best approach to take when embarking on an offshore outsourcing voyage. However, experience has shown that there is one strategy approach that has proven to be the most optimal. This approach is termed the "inside out" strategy.

INSIDE OUT: APPLICATION OUT-SOURCING STRATEGY

The term "inside out" refers to a relatively simple concept:

Use the savings from operational improvements to fund new initiatives that drive top line growth.

Figure 2 below outlines the sequential nature of this approach.

FIGURE 2

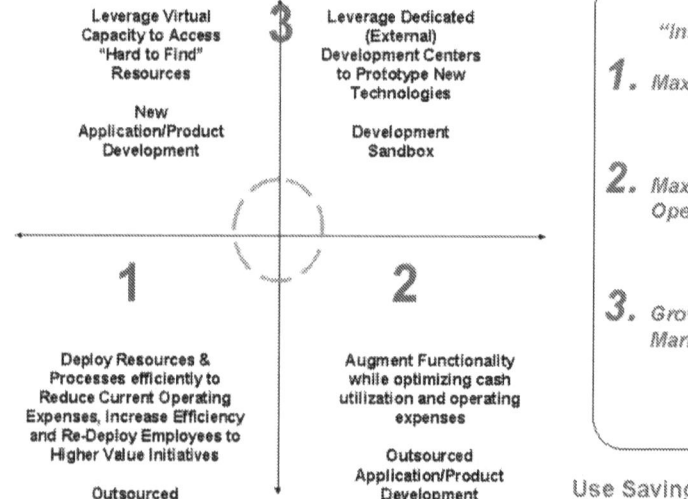

Leverage Virtual Capacity to Access "Hard to Find" Resources

New Application/Product Development

3

Leverage Dedicated (External) Development Centers to Prototype New Technologies

Development Sandbox

1

Deploy Resources & Processes efficiently to Reduce Current Operating Expenses, Increase Efficiency and Re-Deploy Employees to Higher Value Initiatives

Outsourced Application/Product/Version Maintenance

2

Augment Functionality while optimizing cash utilization and operating expenses

Outsourced Application/Product Development [Enhancements/Upgrades of existing Products]

"Inside Out"

1. Maximize ROA

2. Maximize Operating Income

3. Grow Revenue & Market Share

Use Savings from "1" & "2" to fund "3"

THE INSIDE

The term "inside" has many potential meanings. To hard-core IT practitioners, inside could mean the "guts" of operating IT. To a business unit executive it could mean a function that is not market facing. To a CFO, it could mean an initiative that primarily consumes resources, rather than generates them. In the context of offshore application outsourcing, "inside" refers to application maintenance.

STARTING ON THE INSIDE— INCREASED ACCOUNTABILITY

Application maintenance is the most logical place to start a relationship with a new offshore application outsourcer.

Development initiatives historically have a low probability of ever seeing the light of production. Recent studies have indicated that over 75% of application development initiatives exceed original cost estimates and over 50% of application development initiatives are never put into production.

Application maintenance is performed on systems that are already in production. This means that the function of maintaining systems and the processes invoked to perform the function are more predictable. The predictability goes up for IT organizations that have good system documentation and organized ways to measure and continuously improve performance of systems being maintained.

With predictable processes, it will be much easier for you to create rational expectations for outsourcing the maintenance of applications to an offshore partner. Operationally speaking, you can write and put in place a manageable Service Level Agreement (SLA), which increases accountability for both you and your partner.

In the early stages of any relationship, it is important that a foundation of trust is created. In most relationships this foundation is created iteratively—trial, mistake, learning, trial, success, trial, success and so on. Having a predictable process with tangible measures and expectations makes it easier for you and your partner to go through the iterations together. There is no better "bonding" mechanism than joint failure and joint success. The best place to start this experience with an offshore partner is with application maintenance.

STARTING ON THE INSIDE—LOWER RISK

In addition to creating accountability, it can be argued that outsourcing application maintenance carries lower risk than outsourcing application development.

Critics of this contention would argue that if a high percentage of application development initiatives never see the light of day, there is already built-in risk. Why not first outsource development functions to a new offshore partner?

Knowledge acquisition and knowledge transfer are key elements of a partnership with an offshore outsourcer. It is a lot lower risk to have a partner learn the inner workings of an application while they are performing application maintenance. As they perform this function, they get familiar with the code, the interfaces, the business users, the inefficiencies and the opportunities for improvement.

If the first thing a partner does is take on an application development initiative, where the output expected is a new application or an enhancement to an existing application, there is no framework for you to give them guidance. There is a high probability that you are learning at the same time. As such, accountability is difficult (except for time based metrics like meeting release milestones) and therefore risk/exposure is higher.

Development projects in today's economy are selected very carefully. Chances are that your application development initiatives are expected to be of high value to the business and highly strategic. It is high risk to start off a relationship with a new partner by chartering them with something that has limited history and is very high visibility.

STARTING ON THE INSIDE— INCREASED MORALE

As you start working with an outsourcer, your in-house team will expect you to "walk the talk."

You have hopefully positioned this new relationship as one which will allow you to off-load rudimentary (translation: boring) system maintenance work to an offshore partner and re-deploy in-house staff to more strategic endeavors. If you start off by outsourcing the exciting new development initiative to an external partner, your team is bound to be concerned.

As the offshore partner starts the application maintenance work, your team will work closely with the partner to take them through system documentation as well as the formal and informal processes of performing maintenance on the applications. This gives your team a chance to build a productive working relationship with your new partner—

the soft aspects of an offshore voyage that must not be over-looked. Overlooking them can significantly compromise already unstable morale.

STARTING ON THE INSIDE—MORE PROCESS RIGOR

Most offshore application outsourcers have achieved a high degree of process rigor.

The most common measure of process rigor in the IT services industry has become the Carnegie Mellon University, Software Engineering Institute (SEI) Capability Maturity Model (CMM) rating. This scale goes from 1 to 5 (with 5 being the best). CMM Level 5 has become the minimal cost of entry for any offshore outsourcer to have credibility. This is an interesting dynamic since most corporate IT organizations in the U.S. are struggling even to reach CMM Level 3.

Process rigor can be a double-edge sword for an IT organization. If the CMM Level 5 process rigor of your partner is incorporated literally, it could have a detrimental (bureaucratic) impact on your own operations. CMM

Level 5 is documentation and process intense and if you are not prepared for it, it will consume a lot of soft dollars (peoples' time). On the other hand, process rigor is yet another reason why application maintenance is the logical place to start a relationship with an offshore application outsourcer.

As your offshore partner starts the maintenance engagement, they will need to document the application in order to learn how it works. Documentation protocol for the partner will be based on their CMM Level 5 process rigor. Since you own the Intellectual Property (IP) that is in the documentation, and therefore the documentation, you become the beneficiary of the well documented, easily archive-able application IP.

Your offshore partner will also likely put application management processes in place that leverage concepts like a Project Management Office (PMO). Many of the members of this project management office are bound to be Project Management Institute (PMI) certified.

PMI is another institution, similar to the SEI, that grants credentialing (in this case to individuals rather than organizations) for levels of process rigor achieved (in this case for project management rather than software development and maintenance). Concepts like the PMO are rarely in place in corporate IT shops. Emulating these types of management models can provide a lot of process benefits to your IT organization, without overindulging process and creating bureaucracy.

STARTING ON THE INSIDE—RAPID TIME TO MONEY

Application maintenance consumes the lions' share of an IT organization's payroll. If you need to reduce operating costs, the fastest "time to money" can be achieved by addressing the largest bucket of resource consumption first.

Statistics have shown that an offshore partner should be able to maintain your systems for 20-40% below current application maintenance resource consumption levels and should be able to get to this level within 5—9 months of starting the engagement. Obviously, system complexity and size of application portfolio impact these figures, but as a general gauge, they are appropriate.

STARTING ON THE INSIDE— INCREASED ROA

Figure 2 indicates that Quadrant 1 in the matrix allows an IT organization to increase their Return on Assets (ROA). A CIO is often evaluated on their ability to demonstrate a return on the investment made in IT— sometimes called Return on IT (ROIT).

An IT organization produces outputs that are often counted as assets on the balance sheet of an organization. There are two ways for you to increase the ROA. One is to demonstrate increased top line (revenue) growth as a result of the investment in IT. The other way is to decrease your IT resource consumption.

Outsourcing application maintenance to an offshore partner reduces resource consumption and therefore increases the ROA. In addition, the benefits of starting from the "inside" include easier accountability, decreased risk, higher morale, more process rigor and quicker savings.

MOVING HALFWAY TO THE OUTSIDE

Your voyage strategy should start with application maintenance as the first step and quickly move toward the "outside."

Things on the outside are more oriented to application development. However, experience dictates that development of new products and new technologies is not the immediate next step in the offshore voyage. Rather, the logical next step, after application maintenance, is application development in the arena of enhancements/increased functionality for existing applications.

HALFWAY TO THE OUTSIDE—FASTER RAMP-UP

As part of an application maintenance initiative, your offshore outsourcer will become very familiar with all functional and technical aspects of an application.

Application maintenance activities include activities like bug fixes, minor enhancements and application updates. These activities traverse both the application maintenance as well as the application development continuum. The benefit to you is that as you need to increase functionality of your existing applications and perform development-oriented activities such as application/version upgrades, your offshore partner becomes invaluable.

If these development-oriented initiatives were the first ones you chartered your partner with, they would have to spend up-front time learning the application before the actual development work could commence. The history with application maintenance activities allows your partner to speed the "time to market" for introduction of new functionality and application upgrades to your user community.

HALFWAY TO THE OUTSIDE—MORE PROCESS EFFICIENCY

Just as application maintenance initiatives result in more process rigor in your internal IT processes, outsourced application development initiatives result in more efficiency.

As your offshore partner works on modifications, enhancements and upgrades to existing applications, they will follow rigorous processes based on industry standard software development approaches.

By example, if your Enterprise Resource Planning (ERP) financial module requires the latest upgrade to be installed and integrated (a relatively significant development-oriented initiative), the offshore partner might perform what is called a "black box" upgrade. This is a process that is meant to cause minimal disruption to your organization and also optimizes the resources it takes to perform an upgrade of this magnitude. Your partner will take the master files of the financial module and document all interfaces and processes. Then the master files will be taken to the offshore facility where the upgrade to the new version is completed. Testing will be done to ensure that all elements have been incorporated, and the new master files will be shipped back for integration and acceptance testing. This process is extremely organized and is designed such that your business can continue without disruption while the upgrade is being performed.

This type of process efficiency is possible because your partner is already familiar with the way that you use the financial module of your ERP application, from the application maintenance work they have been performing.

HALFWAY TO THE OUTSIDE—BETTER CASH UTILIZATION

As application enhancement requirements surface, an IT organization has two options.

New modules and upgrades can be purchased from software vendors (sometimes accompanied by the professional services teams of the software vendor), or enhancements to existing applications can be made, using the in-house IT team. In the former case, the capital budget is being accessed to make a software purchase, and in the latter case, the in-house team is being used to perform work that is probably maintenance-oriented in nature and not revenue generating.

Using an offshore partner for application maintenance as well as production support and application enhancement allows an IT organization to re-deploy valuable in-house resources to initiatives that might be more strategic (i.e.

revenue generating) in nature. In addition, avoiding a software purchase or using an offshore partner to implement a packaged software upgrade is a good utilization of cash.

Activities such as this are critical to make the journey from the inside out. Essentially, using an offshore partner to perform application maintenance and application enhancement work allows an IT organization to fund new (revenue generating) initiatives from the savings generated.

IT'S NOT THE ONLY WAY

Moving from "the inside out" is not the only way to engage an offshore partner. There are many fruitful, long-term relationships created on the heels of a limited-time application development or staff augmentation relationship. However, this guide is not about luck. It is about taking an organized, proactive approach to offshore application outsourcing. As such, experience shows that a ramp-up of the relationship, starting with application maintenance is the most productive and has the highest likelihood of long term success.

CHAPTER 3

SELECTING THE VOYAGE GUIDE

In the day of Vasco da Gama, sailors often joined the crew of a vessel out of necessity. Economically, there was the promise of riches. Emotionally, there was the promise of adventure and societal recognition—which could lead to riches.

The true reason many sailors signed up for the crew of a da Gama voyage is that there was really no other option. They were trained on the sea, by the sea and they were of the sea. They were eminently un-employable outside of the sea. Choosing the voyage guide was hardly a choice. If a ship were setting sail, they would try to be on it.

In a modern day corporate IT context, the offshore application outsourcing partner choices available are numerous—often too numerous. Ironically, selection of a voyage guide is the most important element of an offshore outsourcing strategy and also the element that is most often bungled.

It is the belief of this author that the primary cause of bungling (PCB) is that the process of partner selection has been made overly complex. The primary cause of the complexity is the never-ending desire for an IT organization to enter analysis-paralysis. Essentially, if the process is not mind-bending, then it must be fluffy. If it is fluffy, it is flawed. This is the curse of the technocrat.

SIMPLICITY IS HIGHLY UNDER-RATED

This chapter will be simple. Not just simple, but also short. As a wise colleague of my often says, "If it does not fit on the back of a business card, it is not worth saying."

Essentially, the most involved part of the offshore outsourcing voyage is, understanding why you want to embark on the voyage and establishing your objectives and strategy for the voyage. Selecting the voyage guide is emotionally challenging, but logistically simple. If the choice of the voyage guide is made rationally, then the rest of the voyage should be straightforward. After all, that is the purpose of a voyage guide—to make the voyage safe, uncomplicated and successful.

This guide assumes that you will follow the simple principles outlined in this chapter, and will be happy with your selection of a voyage guide. If this is the case, the remainder of the voyage is a matter of merely being aware of what will transpire—the rest of the details should be taken care of by the guide and offshore outsourcing partner.

SELECTION CRITERIA-CHECKLIST OR CHOKELIST?

The most flagrant mistake committed by companies seeking an offshore outsourcing partner is to establish a "vendor-client" relationship with the partner.

By definition, a vendor-client relationship implies a hierarchy where the vendor is subservient to the client. One might argue that there are many companies that value their vendors and even go so far as to create awards for vendors that show true partnership characteristics. However, the very use of the word 'vendor' sets the stage for a hierarchical relationship. How many successful marriages begin with a pre-nuptial agreement that is drafted by one spouse and signed off by another? A U.S. based east coast real estate and casino magnet is known for these types of agreements. Enough said.

The selection criteria for a voyage guide should neither be a checklist or a choke-list. The latter is something that companies put in place to create an onerous process for offshore outsourcing providers where only the most willing (translation, the most desperate) offshore outsourcers play. At the end of the process, neither party is truly happy. The offshore outsourcer feels like they had to give too much to get the business, and the company feels like they pulled one over on the vendor—hardly the basis for a fruitful long-term relationship.

If a company utilizes a checklist to ensure that the larger pool of offshore outsourcing companies can be funneled down to a shortlist of "qualified" partners, then a rational selection process can be invoked. This checklist can be viewed as a list of **necessary** characteristics to be included in a final consideration. The list should be rational, not overly lengthy and should invoke Pareto (the 80/20 rule that says that 80 % of the decision can be made with 20%

of the data. However, a checklist is not the end-all, be-all of selecting the voyage guide. There are higher order processes.

SIZE MATTERS

Once a checklist is used to pare down potential partners to a manageable group (3-5) there are two criteria that should be used to reach a final decision. The first one is size and the second is the company structure of the offshore outsourcer.

Size of the voyage guide can be measured in many ways. It can be a measure of revenue, employees, number of customers, number of offices etc. However, like anything, size as a decision-making criterion, requires context to be relevant.

IT'S NOT THE SIZE OF THE SHIP

In the offshore outsourcing world, there are a few companies that have attained significant market repute. In all cases, the driver behind this notoriety has been the performance of the offshore outsourcing company in the equity markets.

There is little doubt that these companies are well managed, and have created a lot of wealth for their shareholders. In fact, many of these companies have outperformed the equity markets overall, year after year, even through the dim years of the quelling of Internet euphoria. These companies are also some of the largest players in the offshore outsourcing market, as measured by revenue or number of offshore employees. However, bigger is not always better. This goes for revenue as well as name recognition.

The problem is that many companies seeking an offshore outsourcing partner gravitate toward these players because of their size and name recognition. There is a sense that if the company is well known and easily recognized, that they would be a natural choice for a voyage guide. This is not always the case.

BOILING THE OCEAN

Let us consider the example of a software company that is attempting to reduce it's overall product development expenses but also, speed time to market for its core revenue generating products.

At first glance, the need seems to be obvious. Partner with an offshore outsourcing company that can provide the necessary (technical) skills in a short timeframe, and can do it for very aggressive labor rates (yielding 30-40% savings from existing levels of expenditure). There is a tendency to gravitate toward larger offshore outsourcers, because they offer the breadth of technical expertise required and can generally offer aggressive rates. However, lets dig deeper.

The head of development of the software company has a need to reduce development expenses by 30% over a six-month period. At the same time, she needs to make sure that the next release of the existing product can be brought to market three months sooner. All this needs to be done while keeping the current version of the product supported, with all showstopper bugs fixed and all platforms supported (including operating systems with Kanji characters!) This is the innovators dilemma (trying to keep the boat afloat while also trying to win the speedboat race) and is akin to being asked to "boil the ocean." In order to do this, she knows she needs to leverage offshore outsourcing. However, the largest player is not the obvious choice.

IS A SMALLER KETTLE EASIER?

As the offshore outsourcer places staff in a capacity to help the software company, the software company is releasing its in-house staff. Hard as this may be, this is the only way to actually reduce cost.

Once the application development work for the new product is complete, there is a need to have staff to maintain the application on an on-going basis. The offshore partner needs to be leveraged for this, since the in-house development staff has been released.

Often, large offshore outsourcing companies rotate their key technical developers from engagement to engagement, in order to leverage the intellect of these talented professionals across multiple clients. For a software company, this could be tragic.

The very people (from the offshore partner) that are most familiar with the application (the ones that have worked on it for the application development initiative) are the ones that will be moved onto other engagements. As a result, all of the undocumented intellectual property (essentially learning) will walk away. The head of development of the software company will have to re-train a cadre of new offshore personnel to take over the application maintenance tasks, which will be time-consuming and resource intensive.

To avoid this situation, it would be best for the software company to establish a (dedicated) virtual capacity center with the offshore outsourcing partner. This is a contractual arrangement where the software company would commit to a minimum number of resources per month as a baseline and in return would be guaranteed that any resources needed above the baseline would be provided to the software company within 'x' period of time. In addition, there would be an agreement that the **exact** individuals that are in the 'baseline' group would be dedicated to the software company as 'adjunct' employees. This makes it a lot easier for the software company to have continuity. This also makes it easier for the offshore outsourcer, because they have predictability of revenue.

The problem is that often, the largest offshore companies are not the most obvious choices for this type of arrangement. Furthermore, the software company might want to set up a model called 'Build-Operate-Transfer (BOT)'— where the resources in the dedicated virtual capacity center can be transferred over to the software company (as employees) after a period of time. Essentially, in a BOT model, the offshore outsourcing company is building a development center for the software company and giving them the option to purchase the development center after a period of time. Is the best choice for this arrangement a large offshore outsourcer?

The scenario outlined above exemplifies how size of offshore outsourcer is not a uni-dimensional selection criterion. It is context sensitive. Sometimes the larger player would have a greater ability to provide resources quickly for an application development initiative. However, the smaller player might be more willing (and therefore able) to contract in a BOT setting and agree to provide the option for their employees to become part of their customers' organization after a period of time. Size matters—especially when you are trying to boil the ocean. However, as with most things, even context sensitive size is not the only criterion.

**Note: the software company example deliberately uses application development as the starting point of the offshore outsourcing partnership. This is meant to demonstrate that the strategy outlined in Chapter 2 is not "the only way."

THE SHAPE OF THE VESSEL

Once you come to terms with the size criteria for your partner, it is also important to consider how the potential partner has structured their business.

At first glance, legal/company structure of the offshore outsourcing company might not seem relevant, but if the legal structure manifests itself in the mechanics of delivering the work (as it usually does), then it matters. Figure 3 below outlines the tradeoffs associated with selecting a voyage guide with a particular legal structure.

FIGURE 3

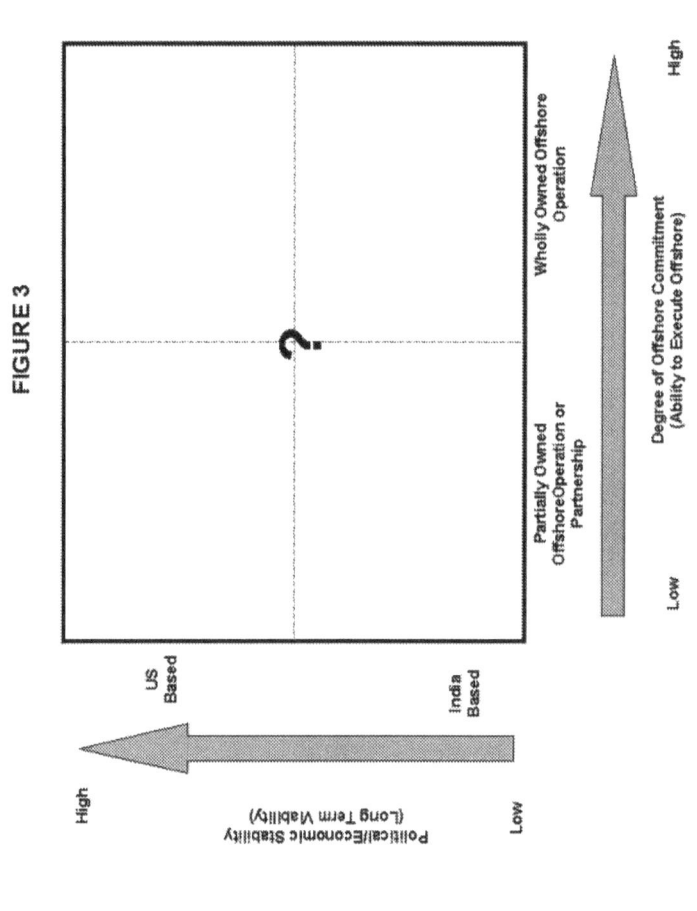

When it comes to legal structure of the potential partner (i.e. shape of the vessel) it is important to note that there are many successful offshore outsourcing companies, with varied legal structures, each with many successful clients.

The purpose of this exercise is not to infuse any pre-conceived notions about the "right" legal structure into your decision-making process. Rather, like most items in this guide, the purpose of the discussion about the shape of the vessel is meant to provide perspective to help you make the right selection of an offshore outsourcing partner.

MADE IN THE USA?

The diagram above, though not an overt endorsement of one particular structure, could seem to imply that a U.S. based company with a wholly owned offshore operation is desirable as an offshore outsourcing partner. This is not the intent. Rather the intent of the matrix is to catalyze you and your organization into considering the tradeoffs of one legal structure over another.

If an offshore outsourcing partner is headquartered/based in the U.S., does that necessarily mean that it is naturally more economically and politically viable? No. However, the delivery model of the U.S. based offshore partner might be a very deliberate mix between on-site (U.S. based and stationed) resources and offshore resources. In which case, the legal structure manifests itself in operational elements that have a potentially positive impact on the success of the partnership.

In the process of delivering work, it is crucial that communication is fluid and issue resolution is rapid. In addition, it is important the there is continuity throughout the partnership, in terms of the people that are "at point" for issue resolution. In other words, the ones accountable for the partnership from the offshore partner company need to be in place for the entire duration of the partnership. A U.S. based company that places U.S. based on-site resources at the client site for the purpose of engagement management, might provide more rapid issue resolution and faster executive access. Then again, they might not. It is worthwhile exploring how the delivery processes of a potential partner mirrors (or is impacted by) their legal structure.

TOURIST OR RESIDENT?

On the dimension of the ownership structure of the offshore operation, the advice in this chapter is a little more prescriptive. A wholly owned offshore operation is a much better choice than one that is a mere partner of the U.S. based or offshore based company.

Strategic business partnerships are fine, but when it comes to a market like offshore technology outsourcing, which is by no means nascent, your partner needs to demonstrate that they are committed to offshore delivery of technology management contracts. A wholly owned offshore operation is one measure of that level of commitment.

Again, context is important. If a wholly owned offshore operation is merely a "shell" and does not manifest itself in fluid communication and delivery processes, then the legal structure is merely for appearances. A wholly owned offshore operation should be so tightly melded with the U.S. organization that the offshore element of a project/engagement for you should be transparent—the interaction between the client and the offshore operation should be transparent to the client.

The 'wholly owned' aspect of the offshore operation should also result in less staff turnover at the offshore location. If the offshore operation is wholly owned, the staff is working for a 'real company.' This means that they are not contract resources waiting on the bench for the next contract. They are salaried employees of a real company, with real benefits, real career growth and a real parent company in the U.S. This should result in more continuity for you in terms of interactions with the partners' staff.

THE MOTION OF THE OCEAN

The criteria discussed above are not the "only way." As emphasized earlier, the relationship with your offshore partner is part science, but mostly art.

Judging the ability of a partnership to work is very much, "gut feel." It is important to not diminish the value of managerial instinct. The analytics outlined in this chapter should not be overlooked, but when it comes to a final decision, no amount of data can compensate for instinct.

The Voyage East can result in denigration or in discovery and conquest. The choice is yours.

0-595-28834-0

www.ingramcontent.com/pod-product-compliance
Lightning Source LLC
Chambersburg PA
CBHW030852180526
45163CB00004B/1548